AN INTRODUCTION TO ORTHODOX SPIRITUALITY

An Introduction to Orthodox Spirituality

by

George Papademetriou

HOLY CROSS ORTHODOX PRESS
Brookline, Massachusetts 02146

Published for

THE GREEK ARCHDIOCESE
YOUTH MINISTRY OFFICE

Fr. Angelo Gavalas, Director

Published by Holy Cross Orthodox Press
50 Goddard Avenue
Brookline, Massachusetts 02146

Cover design by Mary C. Vaporis

ISBN 0-917651-53-7

For

Bishop Gerasimos of Abydos

who taught me

Orthodox spirituality

and

Metropolitan Silas of New Jersey

who suggested the topic

PREFACE

This age of spiritual disarray and confusion in religion and spirituality requires more than an act of intense faith to produce a work such as this by Father George Papademetriou. Religious pluralism has become the defining metaphor of American religious life. Cults and movements have sprung up overnight like exotic mushrooms. Activism, feminism, sexual liberation, and a secularized Christianity — which gives no offense because it will not tolerate the myth of objective revelation — have resolved the ideal of ecumenism by making all Christian traditions equal partners in dialogue. We see around us individual rights exalted as license to do what one pleases. Too many would like to transform the Orthodox Church into a liberated messianic democracy. Truly ours has become an era of liberated fools.

But there are goodly numbers who seek the Risen Savior. With texts such as this, the gospel will be preached ". . . even to the consummation of the world" (Matthew 28.20). Serious seekers of the spiritual life will find this booklet enlightening and enlivening. Christian Orthodoxy is expounded on each page and it behooves the pilgrim to read seriously and make its treasure his own.

I am pleased to recommend to God fearing pious faithful this work that they may grow in grace amd the Spirit of God. In translating its pages into daily living, we will lend a depth of meaning to the whole drama of Orthodox Christianity. The truth it contains will set us free to unite ourselves with the Source of our life and existence and a blessed, rich life will be the reward here and for all eternity.

†NICHOLAS
Bishop of Amissos

THE SOURCES

The sources of Orthodox spirituality are the holy Scriptures, sacred Tradition, the dogmatic definitions of the Ecumenical Synods, and the spiritual teachings of the Greek Orthodox Fathers. Orthodox spirituality is mainly expressed through prayer, daily Christian living, and worship, which ultimately leads to union with the divine uncreated Light.

Man and His Purpose as Creature of God

Before we enter into a discussion of the spirituality of the Orthodox Church, let us see what is man's purpose as a creature of God. Man is created in the image and likeness of God. The human destiny is not to achieve mystical union with the essence of God, but rather to attain moral and spiritual perfection by participation in the divine uncreated energies. Man, according to the Orthodox Fathers, was not created perfect from the beginning. Rather he was created with the potential to achieve perfection through grace. This, of course, was not realized because of the Fall. In the fulness of time, God sent our Lord and Savior Jesus Christ to become man, and through his suffering and resurrection from the dead, restored man to his original state of grace and enabled him to attain perfection. Christ says: "Be perfect as your Father in Heaven is perfect." The ultimate purpose of man, therefore, is to become perfect in God, through love. That is, to attain perfect, selfless love of God and one's fellow human beings.

The Christian Commitment

The life of moral perfection, according to our Bible and the Fathers of the Church, is a call to a life in Christ, that is, a Christlike life. Consequently, the spirituality of the Orthodox Christian is portrayed as a life in Christ, a life of commitment to the Lord, and a complete submission to his will. One lives only to do everything for Christ's sake, as Christ wants it and as Christ would do it.

The Christian commitment to Christ must be made by an inner, free act and is not compelled by any external force, not even by God. "Man is free and able to enter into relations with both kingdoms — the kingdoms of light and that of darkness." These kingdoms, the spiritual and the satanic, are hidden, not in the mind, but much deeper in the soul — "under the mind, beneath the surface of the thoughts," as Saint Makarios asserts. This fourth-century saint already had the notion of "heart," which is strikingly close to the modern psychological concept of the subconscious.

Moral Perfection Is Life in Christ

Orthodox spirituality is described throughout the centuries as life in Christ, striving for moral and spiritual perfection. The mystical union in Orthodox spirituality is not the "devout life" that some sects claim but the communion of the person with God. In sectarian teachings, the "devout life" is a sentimental and emotional relation to "divinity." The Orthodox Church rejects this concept in favor of one which envisions the meeting of man with the divine Person in a mystical way. Orthodox spirituality is union with Christ, with God. A spiritual person is one who purifies himself of all worldly and moral defects in order to be united with the love of Christ. The mystical experience takes place in this world, yet the cause, God, is from beyond the material world. Orthodox spirituality, as well as the whole thought of the Church, is based on the revelation found in the Old and New Testaments. This can be seen by studying the Patristic interpretation of the Christian truths. In the mystical vision of the divine energies of the advanced Christian, he experiences the divine presence within himself, as vision of the uncreated light and of the energies of God. It is especially through the sacrament of the holy Eucharist that we experience mystical union with our Lord.

Philosophy and Divine Knowledge

The important Orthodox doctrine of the incarnation, that is, the divine Logos who became flesh, rendered philosophy and metaphysics irrelevant to our deeper knowledge of the divine truth. Christianity offers access to divine grace for the salvation of mankind through the resurrection of Christ. We cannot speculate about the Logos after the coming of Christ, who is the divine Logos in the flesh, and who sent the Holy Spirit to the world and "teaches us all things." The mystical experience spoken of by the classical

Greeks is abstract and conceptual. That is, in ancient Greek philosophic contemplation, the soul or spirit goes outside the body to be liberated. Philosophy plays only a linguistic role in Orthodoxy, lending the use of its terminology after the terms have been transformed and purified of their secular meanings, "Christianized" philosophy and culture, as Father Georges Florovsky used to say. A master of spirituality, a monk of Mount Athos, describes this point in the following manner: "Many of the Greeks tried to philosophize, but only the monks found and learned the true philosophy." The Logos became flesh and revealed to humanity the divine revelation. He is the Truth and through him we can attain knowledge of the divine will. The metaphysical patterns of the philosophic speculation of the Christian revelation distort the divine mission of the incarnate Logos.

Three Ways Upwards

The Fathers of our holy Church suggest three ways to make progress in the spiritual life and attain spiritual perfection:

1. The way of catharsis or purification
2. The way of illumination, and
3. the way of perfection by total union with God.

These ways can bring the Christian who cooperates with divine grace to perfection. Synergy of the individual effort with the help of the grace of God brings us to our ultimate destiny of perfection. Our Lord's death and resurrection achieve for us our end in attaining the presence of the Holy Spirit within us.

The *Philokalia* speaks of "the increasing knowledge of God decreases knowledge of all else. In other words, the more a man knows God, he knows less of other matters. Not only this, but he begins to realize more and more clearly that neither does he know God." This point is of fundamental importance to Orthodoxy that declares the total mystery and unknowability of the divine essence.

The purpose of man is to achieve moral perfection through the acquisition of the Holy Spirit. In the teachings of Saint Seraphim of Sarov, the Holy Spirit leads the individual through the steps outlined above in order to attain union with the Spirit of Truth.

Monasteries Are Spiritual Centers of Orthodox Spirituality

The spirituality of the Orthodox Church is best exemplified in its spiritual centers, the monasteries. The monk is a "martyr" or "witness" to Christ, the Son of the living God. Dostoyevsky's *The Brothers Karamazov* is an excellent example of this spiritual model in the person of Father Zossima. This monastic model eloquently portrays the spirituality of the Orthodox Church. Dostoyevsky distinguishes between worldly freedom and the spiritual person. He says that the worldly or secular people "maintain that the world is getting more and more united, more and more bound together in brotherly community, as it overcomes distance and sets thoughts flying through the air." But in reality the opposite is true, as is evident in international conflicts and wars. This famous Orthodox novelist expressed eloquently the Orthodox view that in spiritual subjugation, that is, in absolute obedience to Christ, one finds limitless freedom. This is especially exemplified in monasteries where spirituality is nurtured.

The Divine Energies

One of the most important aspects of Orthodox spirituality is participation in the divine energies. Briefly stated, this is an Orthodox doctrine of fundamental importance and very often ignored. In Orthodox theology, a distinction is made between the "essence" and "energies" of God. Those who attain perfection do so by uniting with the divine uncreated energies, and not with the divine essence. The Greek Orthodox Fathers, whenever they speak of God, emphasize the unknowability of God's essence and stress the vision of the divine energies, especially the divine uncreated Light. Orthodox spiritual tradition emphasizes the divine Logos indwelling in the world and our ability to attain a spiritual life and mystical union with the Holy Spirit in this world.

Christian contemplation is not "ecstatic," that is, outside ourselves, but it takes place within the Christian person who is the "temple of the Holy Spirit." The divine energies are "within everything and outside everything." All creation is the manifestation of God's energies. Vladimir Lossky says in the *Mystical Theology of the Eastern Church*: "These divine rays penetrate the whole created universe and are the cause of its existence." The uncreated Light and the knowledge of God in Orthodox tradition "illuminates every man that cometh into this world." It is the same light that the apostles saw on Mount Tabor that penetrates all of creation and transforms it, creating it anew. A modern ascetic says in the *Undistorted Image:* "Uncreated Light is divine energy. Contemplation of Uncreated Light begets, first and foremost, an all-absorbing feeling of the living God — an immaterial feeling of the immaterial, an intuitive, not a rational perception — which transports man with irrestible force into another world, but so warily that he neither realizes when it happens nor knows whether he is in or out of the body." This is not a sentimental or emotional feeling or romantic fantasy. It is experience of the divine uncreated Light described by the neptic Fathers. Again, in the words of the same ascetic: "This supramental sensation of the Living God (which is experienced in contemplation) is accompanied by a vision of light, of light essentially different from physical light. Man himself abides in light because, assimilated to the Light which he contemplates, and spiritualized by it, he then neither sees nor feels his own material being or the materiality of the world."

Illumination

God's act is pure light, and when the Lord appears to us, he always appears as Light. In holy Scripture we read: "In Your Light we shall see light." Only in the state of illumination does divine grace makes possible the contemplation of the divine light. The hidden truths of holy Scripture are not revealed to everyone, since illumination comes through the special divine gift of revelation. For this reason in the early Church, the holy Bible was read only in the Church and only by a charismatic person. In the Orthodox Church, we have never experienced "bibliolatry" or "worship of the Book," as in some sects. The Church holds fast to the unadulterated spirit of the Bible as it was delivered to the Saints, and through them, to us.

Spiritual Warfare

We are saved by Christ and in Christ. Yet we are still subject to temptation and to sin. Therefore, it is important to mention the fact that to acquire spirituality or moral perfection, we must wage war against the "enemy," that is, sin and the devil. Saint Makarios said: "I have not yet seen a perfect Christian man, one completely free (from the devil and sin)." And "although one is at rest in grace and enters into mysteries and revelations and into the sweetness of grace, still sin is yet present within." Consequently, as long as we live, we must be ready to fight against the dark powers of the devil. And "Satan is never quiet from warring. As long as ever a man lives in this world and wears the flesh, he has to war." The holy Bible is the most necessary means of spiritual warfare against the devil; it is also the chief means of acquiring knowledge of the divine will.

The Role of the Sacraments

We must further emphasize the role and purpose of the holy sacraments in attaining spirituality. In the sacraments, we receive divine grace, and in the case of the holy Eucharist, Christ himself, who aids us in waging war successfully against the satanic powers. As Fr. Sergius Bulgakov says: "The heart of Orthodoxy lies in its rites." All the Orthodox rites and sacraments are meant to combat the powers of evil. The sacramental life of the Church is the chief means toward the attainment of spirituality and of ultimate salvation.

The Eucharist as Expression of Spirituality

The question is asked: Is it possible without the holy Eucharist to reach the spiritual state of perfection? The answer is no, because Christ says: "Except you eat the flesh of the Son of Man, and drink his blood, you shall not have life in you." Frequent participation in the most blessed sacrament of the holy Eucharist is the preeminent means for our salvation and spiritual perfection. Jesus said: "for my flesh is meat indeed, and my blood is drink indeed." Thus, Christ's statement makes clear that the "body and blood" of our Lord is necessary for our spiritual perfection. The Eucharist, therefore, is not received merely as an act of obedience to the command of God or of the Church; it is especially an antidote to sin and death. It is a necessary prerequisite for our perfection in our life in Christ. An important interpretation by Saint John Chrysostom makes this clear.

> Paul does not say participation, but communion, because he wishes to express a closer union. For, in receiving holy Communion, we not only participate in Christ, we unite in him. In fact, as this body is united with Christ, so by bread we are united with Christ. But why do I speak of Communion? Paul says that we are identical with this body. For what is this bread? The body of Christ. And what do we become by receiving this bread? The body of Christ: not many bodies, but only one.

The holy Eucharist serves as the bond of unity in love. By the holy Eucharist we are united to Christ and to one another. This is the makeup of the mystical body of Christ: the Church. This concept of the Church as the mystical body of Christ is very dear to our Orthodox tradition because it expresses the reality of Christ in the world and the unity of the Church which is real only when Christ is the central figure. The Orthodox Church rejects the misconception, of sectarian origin, that Christianity is only a system of morals. It strongly emphasizes the fact that mystical union with Christ is a reality in his Church. The whole life of Saint Paul was "a perpetual system of morals in action." Only because of his personal commitment to Christ and his mystical encounter with the divine Lord, did Saint Paul attain spiritual perfection.

Father John of Cronstadt on Teaching Young People the Spiritual Way

In this brief exposition of the vast topic of Orthodox spirituality an introduction was provided only as a beginning to your own investigation of the great truths of our faith. For some this may be regarded as a spiritual discourse not profitable to the ordinary layman. I am convinced, however, that knowledge of the Orthodox tradition of spirituality must be acquired by all Orthodox Christians, especially by those who teach young people and parents. Father John of Cronstadt addressed the teaching priests, the Christian teachers, and leaders in the following penetrating words:

> Do not neglect to uproot from the hearts of children the tares of sins, impure, evil and blasphemous thoughts, sinful habits, inclinations and passions; the enemy and sinful flesh do not spare even children; the seeds of all sins are to be found in the children, too; show them all the danger of sin on the path of life; do not hide sin from them lest through ignorance and want of comprehension, they should be confirmed in sinful habits and attachments, which grow stronger and stronger and bring forth corresponding fruits when children grow up.

These words set forth the mission and goal of the Christian priest, teacher and leader.

Conclusion

In concluding this presentation, the following suggestions can be made to those responsible for the development of spirituality in the Church:

1. In order to transmit Orthodox spirituality to young people, the teacher first must learn it through personal experience and through study of the spiritual writings of Orthodox authors.

2. Each Christian must acquire Orthodox spirituality in his or her own life by living the sacramental life of the Church and by participating frequently in holy Confession and holy Communion.

3. Responsible Christians ought to communicate to young people the great spiritual riches of Christianity and the importance of adhering to the Orthodox tradition of spirituality.

All of us, priests, Church School teachers, leaders, faithful Christians — young and old, and especially parents, have a responsibility to emphasize to young people the importance of their personal commitment to Christ and of their sacramental communion with him. For further spiritual reading and growth especially for youth, an annotated bibliography is provided here. These books are available from Holy Cross Orthodox Bookstore in Brookline.

Selected Bibliography on Orthodox Spirituality

1. Anastasios the Apocrisarios of Rome. *The Life of Our Holy Father Maximus the Confessor.* Trans. Christopher Birehall. Boston, 1982. Pp. 76.

This is a biography of Saint Maximos the Confessor and his struggles for true Orthodox spirituality and correct doctrines. It includes a chronology of the monothelite heresy, maps and places mentioned in the text. Very useful work to understand the spiritual struggle of the saints to hold onto the purity of spirituality.

2. Athanasios. *The Life of Antony and the Letter to Marcellinus.* Trans. Robert C. Gregg. New York, 1980. Pp. 166.

Saint Athanasios was bishop of Alexandria in the fourth century. He was a major figure and a theologian in the christological controversy. He wrote this book to teach other monks the ideal ascetic way of life. The first part of the book is about the life of Antony, a monk who served as an ideal model for the desert monks of Egypt. The second part of the book is about the psalms as prayers for all occasions and for all people. It is written in letter form to Marcellinus so that it is easy to hold the reader's attention.

3. Bloom, Anthony. *Beginning to Pray.* New York, 1970. Pp. 75.

An excellent book for beginners in the art of prayer. Archbishop Anthony Bloom, a Russian monk, gives pointers on how to begin to pray. "The day when God is absent, when he is silent, that is the beginning of prayer." I highly recommend this book; it has a lot to offer beginners.

4. Bloom, Anthony, and LeFebure, Georges, O.S.B. *Courage to Pray.* Trans. Dinah Livingstone. New York, 1973. Pp. 123.

This book is divided into two parts. The first part is written by Archbishop Anthony Bloom, who served as a Russian Orthodox Metropolitan of Great Britain. The second part is written by Georges LeFebure, a Roman Catholic Benedictine monk who served as a member of the French Bishop's committee on Christian unity. The theme of this book is prayer and both authors describe prayer as a dialogue between God and man. It is an excellent book for priests, church school teachers, religious discussion groups, and anyone who seeks to enrich his spiritual life.

5. Kabasilas (Cabasilas), Nicholas. *A Commentary on the Divine Liturgy.* Trans. J. M. Hussey and P. A. McNulty. London, 1977. Pp. 120.

This book is one of Kabasilas' most important works. Kabasilas was a fourteenth-century Byzantine theologian and prominent writer of the time. In his work Kabasilas explains in sequence the events of the celebration of the Divine Liturgy in the Orthodox Church. It also explains the architectural arrangement of the church building. Kabasilas supports all of his comments by quoting the Scriptures. This book is a must for those who want to learn more about the Divine Liturgy.

6. Kabasilas (Cabasilas), Nicholas. *The Life in Christ.* Trans. Carmino J. deCatanzaro. New York, 1974. Pp. 229.

The Life in Christ is one of the most important works of Nicholas Cabasilas. It consists of seven books and sets forth the spiritual life of the Christian. The union with Christ is mediated by the grace of the sacraments and is made fruitful by the cooperation of man. It is an excellent book for the Christian who wants to grow spiritually.

7. Calivas, Alkiviades. *Come Before God.* Brookline, MA., 1986. Pp. 32.

The present small book by the Dean of Holy Cross Greek Orthodox Seminary develops the manner of observance of the holy feasts of the Church. He explains the celebration of the feasts of the Church as means to attaining spirituality.

Observing the days of the Lord and the feasts of the saints helps the Christian to grow in the spirit of Christ. The feast days of the saints and the fast periods of the year are the concrete evidence of the individual response to the Kingdom. Through the observance of the feasts and fasts, each one of us is reminded of Christ's discipleship. The booklet focuses on the liturgical actions which develop the spiritual life of the practicing Christian.

8. Cavarnos, Constantine. *Anchored in God — Life, Art, and*

Thought on the Holy Mountain of Athos. Athens, 1959. Pp. 230.

In this book the author writes his memoirs from his three trips to the Holy Mountain of Athos. He explains the monk's daily life and its relation to the teachings of Christ, Saint Paul, and the Eastern Christian Fathers. The author gives his views on monasticism as well as vivid descriptions of the frescoes, the panel icons, the music, and the architecture of the churches there. I highly recommend this book for those who want to get an inside view of life on Mount Athos.

9. Cavarnos, Constantine. *The Holy Mountain.* Belmont, MA., 1973. Pp. 172.

This book is divided into three parts. Part one is the comprehensive account of the scholarly missionaries and saints of Athos. In part two the author discusses the Athonite music, musicians, and hymnographers. In part three the author makes his own comments about the monks of the Holy Mountain. This book is of much interest for those who want to learn more about the role of monasticism in Orthodox spirituality.

10. Cavarnos, Constantine. *Modern Orthodox Saints. No 7. St. Nectarios of Aegina.* Belmont, MA., 1981. Pp. 222.

This book is the first book in English on Nektarios, a recently canonized saint of the Orthodox Church. It gives information about his life, summarizes his teachings, and gives some selected passages from his publications. It is an excellent biography of a miracle-working saint.

11. Cavarnos, Constantine, and Zeldin, Mary-Barbara. *Modern Orthodox Saints. No. 5. St. Seraphim of Sarov.* Belmont, MA., 1980. Pp. 167.

Saint Seraphim of Sarov is a modern saint in the Orthodox Church. This book contains his messages, his teachings, and gives information about his life as a mystic, a healer, and a comforter. It also contains the conversations with his disciple, Motorilov. Those who are concerned about their spiritual life as well as those who are interested in cultural information about Russia can benefit by reading this book.

12. Archimandrite Chrysostomos. *The Ancient Fathers of the*

Desert. Vol. 1. Brookline, MA., 1980. Pp. 118.

The present text is a translation from the *Evergetinos* on the passions and perfection in Christ. It contains excellent spiritual counsels and direction. It gives numerous examples of holy men who struggled to attain spiritual heights. Very important book for those who seek to learn and practice the Christian struggle for perfection.

13. Archimandrite Chrysostomos. *The Ancient Fathers of the Desert.* Vol. 2. Brookline, MA., 1986. Pp. 90.

This volume contains stories and examples of Christian spiritual living from early and contemporary Orthodox Christians. The narrative is like a story that gives rich spiritual teaching and proper direction for spiritual people to follow. Real people with flesh and blood learn to live under the power of the Lord and in the presence of Christ.

14. Colliander, Tito. *The Way of the Ascetics.* Trans. Katharine Ferre. London, 1960. Pp. 123.

This book is very short and easy to read. It is based on the sayings of the Holy Fathers of the Orthodox Church and has a lot of first-hand spiritual quotations from their writings. It is written not for the monk or nun but for the lay Christian in simple language. It gives a lot of valuable information on prayer, fasting, how to cultivate the virtues, and how to fight evil. I highly recommend this book for lay people who want to learn more about Orthodox spirituality, especially if they are involved in Bible study.

15. Costa, Francis, ed. *God and Charity: Images of Eastern Orthodox Theology, Spirituality, and Practice.* Brookline, 1979. Pp. 103.

There is a collection of six articles in this book. Five of them are by Orthodox writers and one is by a Roman Catholic writer. Each article gives the author's point of view and what his church believes about the particular topic under discussion. The last lecture, by Robert G. Stephanopoulos, brings out some of the current relations between the Orthodox Church and the Roman Catholic Church.

16. *The Desert Fathers.* Trans. Helen Waddell. Ann Arbor, MI., 1960. Pp. 209.

In this jewel of a book, the most enticing of all medieval texts have been put together for our edification. It quotes many "apophthegmata," or spiritual sayings of the Desert Fathers of Egypt. It also includes the lives of Saint Paul the First Hermit, Saint Mary of Egypt, and Saint Pelagia. It is a very valuable work.

17. Dorotheos of Gaza. *Discourses and Sayings.* Trans. Eric P. Wheeler. Kalamazoo, MI., 1977. Pp. 259.

The main motive of Dorotheos in writing these discourses was to educate his fellow monks. He writes in a didactic way and his main focus is morality. He is the ideal spiritual master to introduce the Orthodox Christian into the rich spiritual universe of the deserts of Egypt, Palestine, and Syria. The Discourses are full of humanity and psychological insight. In this book, one can find a spiritual guide to the pure Christian life.

18. Dudko, Dmitrii. *Our Hope.* Trans. Paul D. Garrett. Crestwood, New York, 1977. Pp. 292.

This book contains the invaluable sermons of Fr. Dudko preached in Russia to counteract the anti-religious propaganda of the Soviet Communists and to promote Orthodox spirituality. It is a witness to the Orthodox Christian courage to preach and live the message of Christ and Orthodoxy even if it costs one's life. The sermons answer questions of people of various religious backgrounds — Christians, Jews, Muslims, Buddhists, etc. and even atheists and communists. His approach is instructive and apologetic in nature.

19. Fedotov, G.P. ed. *A Treasury of Russian Spirituality.* London, 1952. Pp. 501.

An historical treatment of the spirituality of the Orthodox Church in Russia is found here. It includes the lives of Russian saints from the eleventh to the twentieth century and describes the long tradition of spirituality in Russia from its roots to the present day. It is an informative book for those who want to know more about the Church in Russia and Orthodox spirituality.

20. Gillet, Fr. Lev. *In Thy Presence.* Crestwood, NY., 1977. Pp. 144.

This work contains meditations which are written in the form of God speaking to the reader. There are also meditations on the presence of Christ in our lives. The actions of our daily lives, which often threaten to become a meaningless routine, are considered one by one. It is easy to read and I recommend it for Christians of all ages.

21. Gregerson, Jon. *The Transfigured Cosmos: Four Essays in Eastern Orthodox Christianity.* New York, 1960. Pp. 111.

This book presents the Orthodox spiritual tradition in four essays. It deals with icons, Orthodox worship, spiritual life, and the mystical tradition of the Orthodox Church. It also deals with Russian religious life, the hesychast spiritual traditionm and the invocation of the sacred name of Jesus. It also gives a selected bibliography for further reading in Orthodox spirituality.

22. Harakas, Stanley S. *The Melody of Prayer: How to Personally Experience the Divine Liturgy.* Minneapolis, MN., 1979. Pp. 39.

The Melody of Prayer is a short book which gives practical advice on how one can personally experience the Divine Liturgy. It discusses the thoughts, practice, and bodily participation one should have during the Divine Liturgy. Harakas calls the whole worship service a "melody of prayer." This short, easy to read book is a useful guide to read before and after the Divine Liturgy to understand what takes place and how to participate in it.

23. Hopko, Thomas. *The Spirit of God.* Wilton, 1976. Pp. 124.

The purpose of this book is to enrich the knowledge and increase the awareness of the Orthodox Christian about the Holy Spirit. It contains excerpts from the great Fathers and theologians of the Orthodox Church. An important introduction to the doctrine of the Holy Spirit and theological and spiritual sources of Orthodoxy.

24. John Klimakos. *The Ladder of Divine Ascent.* Trans. Lazarus Moore. London, 1952. Pp. 270.

This is one of the most treasured handbooks of the spiritual life. It is a description of the steps upwards to heaven; that is, to spiritually elevate and attain spiritual maturity. It gives instructions of solitary life, prayer, struggle against evil thoughts and temptations, and the spiritual qualities of a spiritual master. This book is greatly loved by Greek and Slavic monastics. It is also very helpful for the modern person who seeks spiritual guidance in the turmoil of the world.

25. Krivocheine, Basil. *In the Light of Christ; St. Symeon the New Theologian: Life, Spirituality, Doctrine.* Trans. Anthony P. Gythiel. Crestwood, NY, 1986. Pp. 411.

This authoritative work places Saint Symeon the New Theologian(949-1022) in the tradition of the great spiritual masters of Orthodoxy. Saint Symeon stresses the reality of his personal encounter with Christ and the Holy Spirit. It is an excellent guide for those seeking spiritual renewal.

26. Lossky, Vladimir. *In the Image and Likeness of God.* New York, 1974. Pp. 232.

This is a collection of essays by the late prominent Orthodox theologian Vladimir Lossky. They were selected and arranged before his death. These articles are of diverse themes but synthesize Lossky's theological thought and vision. It presents a consistent doctrinal statement of Orthodox understanding of man's destiny as communion in love with the triune God.

27. Lossky, Vladimir. *The Mystical Theology of the Eastern Church.* London, 1957. Pp. 252.

This book is a scholarly work that speaks both to the Orthodox theologian as well as to the non-Orthodox theologian. It explains theological topics such as dogmatics, monasticism, mystical experiences, comparative theology, Christian anthropology, and sociology. This book can serve as a guide for the person who wants to study Orthodox theology as well as for the person who wants to live a better spiritual life.

28. Lossky, Vladimir. *The Vision of God.* Trans. Asheleigh Moorhouse. London, 1963. Pp. 139.

This is a study of the meaning of the vision of God and its impact on the life and thought of the Orthodox Church and individual Christian. It contains essays on the patristic view of spiritual vision from the Christian beginnings to the time of Saint Gregory Palamas, a fourteenth-century theologian. It shows how the Fathers provide a purpose and goal for the Christian life, both proclaiming and anticipating the kingdom of heaven.

29. Makarios the Starets of Optino. *Russian Letters of Direction, 1834-1860.* Trans. Iulia de Beausobre. Westminster, 1947. Pp. 108.

This book contains eight meditations on the Beatitudes. It is a very good and useful guide to understand the message of the Beatitudes and to implement Christ's teaching in our lives. It is very good reading for all who seek to attain a richer spiritual life.

30. Georgios I. Mantzaridis. *The Deification of Man: St. Gregory Palamas and the Orthodox Tradition.* Trans. from the Greek by Liadain Sherrard. Crestwood, NY., 1984. Pp. 137.

Professor Mantzaridis examines the theological understanding of deification. He emphasizes theosis or deification, properly understood, in the eschatological and ineffable communion with Christ and the divine energies. This is participation of the believer in the kingdom of God. It is the experience and communion of the uncreated light that Christ revealed to his apostles on Mount Tabor, an ontological participation in the uncreated nature of God.

31. Maximos the Confessor. *The Church, the Liturgy and the Soul of Man.* Trans. Dom Julian Stead. Still River, MA., 1982. Pp. 120.

The present work is a brilliant work on the relation of Church, Liturgy, and the soul of man as reflected in the Orthodox Church. It is very interesting reading in which the liturgical image penetrates the entire universe and especially man's life in the world. The translator did a superb job of communicating the original doctrines in simple and readable English.

32. Meyendorff, John. *St. Gregory Palamas and Orthodox Spirituality.* Crestwood, NY., 1974. Pp. 184.

This book was written by a prominent Orthodox scholar and examines the spiritual doctrines of Orthodoxy as related to the life and theology of Saint Gregory Palamas. It presents the spiritual tradition of Orthodoxy from early Christianity, through the patristic and Byzantine periods, to the present day.

33. A Monk of the Eastern Church. *The Prayer of Jesus.* Revised edition with a foreword by Bishop Kallistos Ware. Crestwood, NY., 1987. Pp. 120.

The present work discusses the origin and practice of the Jesus Prayer in the Orthodox Church. This unique study provides the reader with both an historical and spiritual understanding of the prayer of the invocation of the name of Jesus. It gives the scriptural and patristic origins of prayer. An excellent spiritual reading and meditation.

34. A Monk of the Eastern Church. *A Day with Jesus.* New York, 1964. Pp. 109.

This work is divided into forty-six brief meditations based on gospel texts and scenes. They are presented in a manner that suggests direct contact with the soul of our divine Savior. It is a good book for those seeking spiritual growth.

35. A Monk of the Eastern Church. *On the Invocation of the Name of Jesus.* London, 1960. Pp. 32.

This short work has a practical purpose, to help Christians in the world and monks who desire to follow the "way of the Name." It is a collection of meditations for the inner enrichment of the seeker. It is written in simple language as a guide to spirituality, avoiding technical theological language. It is intended for the simple folk who seek to grow spirituality, avoiding technical theological language. It is intended for the simple folk who seek to grow spiritually in this world.

36. A Monk of the Eastern Church. *Orthodox Spirituality — An Outline of the Orthodox Ascetical and Mystical Tradition.* London, 1957. Pp. 103.

The spiritual life is presented in this book in the light of the doctrines and sacraments of the Orthodox Church. The spirituality presented here is that of the Fathers of the Church and the long Orthodox tradition that is not limited to one country or nationality. This work is very important to understand Orthodox spirituality.

37. Nikodemos of the Holy Mountain and Makarios of Corinth. *The Philokalia.* London, 1979. Pp. 378; vol. 2, 1981, pp. 414; vol. 3, 1984, pp. 379.

The Philokalia is a collection of texts written between the fourth and fifteenth centuries by spiritual masters of the Orthodox tradition. First published in Greek in 1782, translated into Slavonic and later into Russian, the *Philokalia* has exercised an influence far greater than that of any other book in the recent history of the Orthodox Church.

38. Papademetriou, George C. *Introduction to St. Gregory Palamas.* New York. Pp. 103.

"The author gives an introduction of the life and works of Saint Gregory Palamas, a fourteenth-century theologian. It deals mostly with the energies and essence of God. It is a very good book for people who are interested in Palamite theology and for the lay person who is interested in learning about Palamas and his teachings. I highly recommend this book to the Orthodox Christian who is interested in improving his spiritual life. It can also be of tremendous value in seminary classes or theology classes in secular universities."

39. Papadopoulos, Gerasimos. *Orthodoxy: Faith and Life: Christ in the Gospels.* Vol. 1. Brookline, MA., 1980. Pp. 164.

The life in Christ is experienced in the personal relation with Christ in the Gospels. Bishop Gerasimos wrote these two volumes as a result of his lifelong experience of Christ's presence in his life. The Gospels are the presence of Christ in the world. This is an excellent book to guide one in his or her Christian growth and spiritual perfection in Christ. The story of Christ is told from the heart by one who lives and breathes his divine and eternal truth.

40. Papadopoulos, Gerasimos. Orthodoxy: *Faith and Life: Christ in the Life of the Church,* Vol. 2 Brookline, MA., 1986, Pp. 156.

The purpose of this work is to help Christians to gain deeper knowledge of the life in Christ. Doctrine, worship, and Christian practice are united in the Orthodox Church as an experience of salvation in Christ. Christians are called to transform themselves and the world into the kingdom of God. In this second volume, Bishop Gerasimos portrays Christ as the apostles and church Fathers knew him and lived by his words in the Church.

41. Poulos, George. *Orthodox Saints.* Brookline, MA., Vol. 1, 1976, pp. 200; Vol. 2, 1978, pp. 202; Vol. 3, 1980, pp.208; Vol. 4, 1982, pp. 200.

The lives of the Saints are models for us to live a spiritual life. These four volumes are excellent spiritual daily readings. The lives of the men and women who lived and died for Christ thoughout the ages are an inspiration for us today. The saints above all loved Christ and their lives exemplified this in word and in action. The four volumes by Father Poulos include the biographies of over four hundred heroes of the Church whose lives deserve to be known and imitated by all Christians.

42. Schmemann, Alexander. *Great Lent.* Crestwood, NY., 1969. Pp. 124.

This book is well-written and easy to understand even for the average lay person. It gives an excellent analysis of the Bible readings relating to Great Lent and, through vivid descriptions, gives the reader the opportunity to attend the lenten services and discover for himself the liturgical tradition. The book encourages every Orthodox Christian to participate in church life.

43. Schmemann, Alexander. *For the Life of the World: Sacraments and Orthodoxy.* New York, 1963. Pp. 86.

The famous Orthodox theologian, Fr. Alexander, wrote this book as a study guide for students. Its purpose is to guide the reader to an Orthodox approach to the world and liturgical experience. It explains life in the sacraments and mission of Orthodox Christian life in the world.

44. Schmemann, Alexander. *For the Life of the World.* Crestwood, NY., 1973. Pp. 151.

This book is a revision and expansion of the above. The emphasis is on liturgical experience in the world and the sacramental life as a way to grow in Orthodox spirituality. An important reading in understanding the spiritual life in the Orthodox Church.

45. Sjogren, Per-Olof. *The Jesus Prayer: Lord Jesus Christ, Son of God, have mercy upon me.* Philadelphia, 1975. Pp. 96.

This book shows the tradition and spiritual background of this simple prayer. It is written for people from all walks of life. It is about the "prayer of the heart" as practiced in Sinai, Mount Athos, and Russia. The purpose of this book is to deepen spirituality and to further nurture fellowship and union with Christ in love and prayer. It is a guide in living the Christian message in the midst of our world and society today.

46. Sergieff, John Iliytch. *My Life in Christ* or *Moments of Spiritual Serenity and Contemplation, of Reverent feeling, of earnest self-amendment, and of peace in God.* Trans. E. E. Goulaeff. Jordanville, NY., 1957. Pp. 298.

This is a biography of Fr. John and includes sections on his early life, his education, and his ministry as a priest. Sergieff gives useful instructions for spiritual growth through the reading of Scripture, religious books, and especially sacraments and prayer. It is a very good guide for those who seek to live a spiritual life.

47. Sofrony, Archimandrite. *The Undistorted Image. Staretz Silouan: 1866-1938.* London, 1958. Pp. 207.

This book is a biography of a Russian peasant who went to Mount Athos in 1892 to live a spiritual life until his death in 1938. He was unlearned, but left several important spiritual sayings which his spiritual son, Archimandrite Sofrony, gathered, edited and published in this volume. This book can help the reader better understand Orthodox spiritual life.

48. Stylianopoulos, Theodore. *The Gospel of Christ.* Brookline, MA., 1981. Pp. 31.

Orthodox spirituality is contained in holy Scripture. The present brief work by an Orthodox Scripture scholar is an excellent interpretation of the spiritual message of Christ. It is a book that gives spiritual direction to contemporary Christians to live a life according to the gospel of Christ.

49. Stylianopoulos, Theodore. *Bread for Life — Reading the Bible.* Brookline, 1980. Pp. 94.

The purpose of this book is to introduce a person to the message of the Bible as one of the great spiritual resources of our Orthodox tradition. It gives practical tips on how to study the Bible in private and in a group. It also explains the relation of the Bible and the Divine Liturgy and gives useful information on current English translations of the Bible.

50. Stylianopoulos, Theodore. *Christ in our Midst: Spiritual Renewal in the Orthodox Church.* Brookline, 1981. Pp. 75.

This book is short and simple. It is a very useful book for a Bible study group because it gives the Orthodox point of view on spiritual renewal. It has numerous quotations from the Desert Fathers to support the discussions. I recommend this book for beginners and advanced readers alike who are interested in Orthodox spirituality.

51. Symeon the New Theologian. *The Discourses.* New York, 1980. Pp. 396.

This work consists of thirty-six discourses which Symeon preached to his monks. Some of the spiritual themes which are covered are repentance, detachment, renunciation, charity, impassibility, remembrance of death, sorrow for sins, the practice of God's commandments, mystical union with the indwelling Trinity, faith, and contemplation. In this book Symeon speaks about his vision of God and says that everyone has the ability to see God if he lives and practices a true spiritual life.

52. Trakatellis, Demetrios. *Growing in the Knowledge of Christ.* Brookline, MA., 1987. Pp. 18.

The present booklet by Bishop Demetrios is an excellent presentation on spiritual growth. It is especially very good for youth and young adults in order to be guided to grow spiritually. Through knowledge of Christ, one grows spiritually. His Grace points out that one must be transfigured to be united with Christ and to become a Christ-like person. The message of Christ and the Church is articulated in this booklet in order to communicate it to the present generation.

53. Vaporis, Nomikos M. *Father Kosmas the Apostle of the Poor.* Brookline, 1977. Pp. 164.

This volume presents the life and writings of Saint Kosmas the Aitolian who died a martyr's death. His spiritual sayings were recorded by his disciples and constitute great spiritual reading, especially on the topics of love, sharing, and prayer.

54. *The Way of a Pilgrim* and *The Pilgrim Continues His Way.* Trans. R. M. French. New York, 1965. Pp. 242.

The Way of a Pilgrim is an excellent work on Orthodox spirituality. Its main theme is prayer. The author is anonymous, but the time is the nineteenth century and the place is Russia. The book is about the experiences of a Russian pilgrim who is journeying everywhere to find out what the "prayer of the heart" is about. The book is so moving that the reader can actually share a religious experience with the pilgrim. It is considered a classic of spiritual life and is recommended for every Orthodox Christian as a guide to his or her spiritual growth.

55. *Writings from the Philokalia: On Prayer of the Heart.* London, 1951. Pp. 420. *Early Fathers of the Philokalia.* London, 1954.

These two volumes contain a collection of spiritual writings by Church Fathers of the Orthodox Church from the fourth to the fourteenth century. It is a description of the spiritual life by Fathers who reached the highest level of spirituality to lead people to theosis and spiritual knowledge. An excellent guide to attain unceasing prayer and spiritual perfection.